WHAT'S WORTH FIGHTING FOR?

What's Worth Fighting For in Your School?
Michael Fullan and Andy Hargreaves

What's Worth Fighting For in the Principalship?
Michael Fullan

What's Worth Fighting For "Out There"?
Michael Fullan and Andy Hargreaves

What's Worth Fighting for in the Principalship

Michael Fullan
Foreword by Roland S. Barth

Teachers College
Columbia University
New York and London

Published in Canada as *What's Worth Fighting For in the Principalship? Strategies for Taking Charge in the School Principalship, Second Edition,* by Ontario Public School Teachers' Federation.

Published by Teachers College Press, 1234 Amsterdam Avenue, New York, NY 10027

ISBN 0-8077-3705-4

Printed on acid-free paper

Manufactured in the United States of America

10 09 08 07 06   6 7 8 9 10 11

Contents

Foreword

A principal I know, in addressing her faculty one afternoon, made a slip—I guess it was a slip—and assured her group, "At this school we live on the bleeding edge."

These are indeed tough times for public education and for public educators. Many have come to question what they and their schools stand for. Many experience an erosion in commitment to whatever that is. And many, in one way or another, are giving up.

In this often bleak context, I find much welcome, good news within the covers of this tidy little volume:

Public schools and their leaders stand for a great deal.

What they stand for is of sufficient importance to not only acknowledge but to fight for.

There are many ways to fight successfully.

It is the school leader who must not only engage in but lead the fight.

The tough news for would-be school-based reformers is that there is no silver bullet in these pages or elsewhere. Rather, the bottom line is captured by a bumper sticker I once saw, "You can't lead where you won't go." Mahatma Gandhi put it more prosaically: "We must *be* the change we want to see in the world." To change schools we must change ourselves. More specifically, we must undergo a huge paradigm shift from, as they say in the research university, being the dependent variable to becoming the independent variable.

Schools and school systems are unsuccessful at many things. One area in which they excel is in promoting a culture of dependency. "What am I supposed to do?" the superintendent must ask of the local and state boards. Then memos go out to principals who respond, "What am I supposed to do?" Principals, in turn, put memos in teachers' boxes—or in their e-mail. Teachers respond, "What am I supposed to do?" Teachers in turn put assignments on pupils' desks which are greeted by students with, "What am I supposed to do?" And so it goes. This is a pathological pattern, Michael Fullan persuasively argues, worth fighting *against.*

The words you are about to encounter will exhort you to become the independent variable, to come into close touch with what you stand for, and then to muster the courage and the imagination to stand there. This is an idea worth fighting for.

In what follows you will find ten unusual and valuable guidelines for making this personal and professional transformation. They are worth fighting for.

I made good use of the previous edition of *What's Worth Fighting For in the Principalship?* in courses I taught at Harvard. I wish I had had access to these insights during my own turbulent years as a school principal. I find this second edition offers even more: more insights and details for schoolpeople from this "critical friend" in academia, and more emphasis that a lifelong career as a leader necessarily entails a lifelong career as a learner—a "perpetual learner," the author says. Indeed, especially in our profession, one is a learner and *thereby* a leader.

You will learn much from this volume about where it is possible for a school and a school leader together to go, and about different routes to get there. Most of all you will learn that "You *can* lead where you *will* go." Another idea worth fighting for!

Roland S. Barth
Founding Director, The Principals' Center
Harvard Graduate School of Education

Preface

Overload Fosters Dependency

The original edition of this book, published by the Ontario Public School Teachers' Federation, was the first in what turned out to be a trilogy of books designed to help teachers and principals fight for fundamentally positive changes that will benefit themselves and their students.

This new edition updates the argument that the answer lies in seeking deeper insights and corresponding action guidelines which are more accessible to the leaders themselves. Distant system solutions are not of much use to the leader who yearns to make positive improvements in the face of great complexity.

The premise in this book is that the "system," however unwittingly, fosters dependency on the part of the principals. Sometimes the pressure for dependency comes from below, as in teacher expectation; sometimes it comes from above, as in school board directives. Paradoxically, dependency is fostered both by emphasis on tradition and by demands for innovation. The role of principals in implementing innovations is more often than not a case of being on the receiving end of externally initiated changes. Dependency is created through the constant bombardment of new tasks and continual interruptions on the job which keep principals occupied or at least off balance. Overload fosters dependency. Principals are either overloaded with what they are doing or overloaded with all the things they think they should be doing. Ironically, management books which profile leadership solutions often make matters worse by keeping leaders dependent on the latest techniques. Dependency, I will argue, may also be internalized or too easily tolerated by principals themselves.

By "dependency," I mean that one's actions are predominantly shaped, however unintentionally, by events and/or by actions or directions of others. Empowerment, taking charge and otherwise playing a central role in determining what is to be done, are the opposite of dependency. Taking charge does not mean that one eschews interdependencies. As will become clear, effective empowerment and interdependency go hand in hand.

While I make the case that principals must take charge of their own destiny, I explicitly reject any notion of isolated autonomy. Indeed, the empowered, interdependent principal has, and experiences, great social responsibilities to act. Empowerment and accountability, far from being polar opposites, are intimately related. The empowered principal working collaboratively is far more responsible than the dependent principal. Dependency is closer to helplessness than it is to responsiveness. The message in this monograph is that individual principals, with or without help, must transcend the problem of dependency if it is to be resolved, and hence, if principals are to be effective. This need has become all the more urgent as the weakening of intermediate agencies (like the local school board) gives way to expectations for greater self-management for schools.

This book pursues the problem of dependency and makes recommendations for how to overcome it. Chapter one starts with a description of how bad things are. I call this situation the "nonrational" world of the principal, borrowing a term from Patterson, Purkey and Parker (1986). More recently, one can just as accurately draw on chaos theory to portray the nonlinear, dynamically complex reality of today's school leaders (Fullan, 1993). There are two key points in these new analyses. First, in the conclusion that the "system" is inherently, ineluctably, hopelessly nonlinear. In other words, this is the nature of the beast. It is for this reason that "if only" statements are not very productive starting points for making headway. Second, within chaos and nonrationality are *patterns* which form periodically or can be helped to form. Here is where the leader as learner is absolutely crucial. It is only perpetual learners that can cope with, make sense of, and indeed help forge meaning out of changing situations.

In the second chapter, "New Conceptions of Leadership," the point of departure is that the present system simply is not working, and that new management theories and techniques either are wrong-headed, or, if on the right track, take us only so far—tantalizingly close to breakthroughs, but not really helpful for day to day action. Case examples are provided to illustrate what these more effective actions might look like taking, "advocacy and resistance," "whole system reform," and "school councils" as cases in point. New conceptions of the principalship combine the moral purpose of leadership with the disposition and skills of effective change agents.

The heart of the book is embedded in the title "Guidelines for Action" formulated in chapter three. These guidelines help principals break the cycle of dependency both for themselves and for those with whom they work. While I focus on the principal, the ideas are equally applicable to teacher leaders. Indeed the effective principal and the effective teacher leader must go together, as the entire trilogy makes clear.

The other two books in the series reinforce and extend the analysis and guidelines for action outward. In *What's Worth Fighting For in Your School?* my colleague Andy Hargreaves and I examine the culture of the school, starting with the observation that schools are not now learning organizations either for students or for teachers. We discuss four types of school cultures—fragmented individualism, balkanization, contrived collegiality, and collaboration: only the latter has potential for continuous learning. We provide ideas for principals and teachers to change the current situation. Eight guidelines for principals and twelve for teachers lay out some of the core starting points and most powerful levers for change.

In *What's Worth Fighting For "Out There"?* (forthcoming), Hargreaves and I conclude that we must reframe the relationship between those in the school and those outside it. This book clearly indicates that in a world of growing complexity and rapid change, if we are going to bring about significant improvements in teaching and learning within schools, we must forge strong, open, and interactive connections with communities *beyond* them. To do this, we must go "wider" by developing new relationships with parents, employers, universities, technology, and the broader profession. We must also go "deeper" into the heart of our practice, by rediscovering the passion and moral purpose that makes teaching and learning exciting and effective. The closing, "Guidelines for Action," for principals and for teachers in *What's Worth Fighting For "Out There"?* shows just what it means to go wider and deeper in this way.

Educational reform has failed time and time again. We believe that this is because reform has either ignored principals and teachers or oversimplified what they do. And educators themselves have not yet taken the initiative to build the new conditions necessary for reversing a trend that has overburdened schools with problems, and ironically has added insult to injury by overloading them with fragmented, unworkable solutions.

The WHAT'S WORTH FIGHTING FOR? trilogy establishes a new mindset and a series of guidelines that enable principals and teachers to obtain greater understanding of the way things are, and, above all, provides them with concrete ideas for changing things for the better—ideas that are within their own control.

What's Worth Fighting for in the Principalship

Chapter 1

The Nonrational World of the Principal

How Bad are Things for the Principal?

*Despite all the attention on the principal's leadership role
we appear to be losing ground, if we take as our measure
of progress the declining presence of increasingly large
numbers of highly effective, satisfied principals.*

The current picture presents a serious problem if one considers the
cumulative and ever-increasing expectations being placed on principals. One early example was presented in a study of 137 principals
and vice-principals in the Toronto Board of Education (EduCon,
1984). In this work several measures indicated the problem of overload. Respondents were asked to rate 11 major expectations (e.g.,
new program demands, number of Board priorities and directives,
number of directives from the Ministry, etc.) in terms of whether
the expectation had increased, decreased, or remained the same in
the previous five years. On the average, across all 11 dimensions,
90% of the principals/vice-principals reported an increase in
demands, with only 9% citing a decrease.

Principals and vice-principals reported a number of specific
major additions to their responsibilities referring to new initiatives
in teacher appraisal, curriculum plans, and multicultural programs.

In response to a direct question, no one could think of a responsibility that had been "removed." Some "reduction" was mentioned
in teacher hiring, due to declining enrolment. Time demands, as
might be expected, were listed as having increased in dealing with
parent and community groups (92% said there was an increase),
trustee requests (91%), administration activities (88%), staff
involvement and student services (81%), social services (81%), and
board initiatives (69%). Parents, trustees, consultants, and teachers
who were asked all confirmed that there were greater time and program demands on principals over the past five years. There was one

other finding about expectations and demands: principals did not object to many of the new responsibilities per se. In fact, the majority saw value in a lot of new programs. They were concerned more with the complexity and time demands involved in implementing the new procedures than the procedures themselves.

Principals and vice-principals were also asked about their perceptions of effectiveness. Remarkably, in light of the fact that it is a self report, 61% of the respondents reported a *decrease in principal effectiveness*, with only 13% saying it was about the same, and 26% reporting an increase. An identical percentage (61%) reported decreases in "the effectiveness of assistance ... from immediate superiors and from administration." The list goes on: 84% report a decrease in the authority of the principal, 72% a decrease in trust in the leadership of the principal, and 76% a decrease in principal involvement in decision-making at the system level. On the question, "Do you think the principal can effectively fulfill all the responsibilities assigned to him/her?" 91% responded, "No."

Almost a decade and half later, one could add scores of other expectations involving site-based management, school-business links, standards' assessment. Indeed, it is no longer a matter of additive overloads. The definition of the very job of the principal has undergone fundamental change.

Evans (1996) notes there have always been chronic tensions in leadership: between managing and leading; between resources and demands; between being a leader but being dependent on others; and between being isolated but in a fishbowl. What is new, Evans observes, is the 'extent and intensity' (p. 152):

> The changing nature of organizational life has exacerbated these chronic conflicts to the point of disempowering leaders and diminishing the quality of their lives. (p. 153)

This explosion of demands on leaders, argues Evans, "decreases school leaders' sense of efficiency and heightens their feelings of isolation, insecurity, and inadequacy." (p. 156)

Virtually all of the principals and superintendents that Evans encountered "acknowledge that their professional lives have grown more complicated and less satisfying," leading many to question not just whether it can be done, but also whether it is worth the cost. (p. 156)

Conservative Tendencies in the Principalship

While the situation in and of itself is daunting, it may be aggravated by historically conservative tendencies in the principalship. I speak here not of official policies or expectations, but of more hidden tendencies that inhibit sustained attention to change. Sarason (1982) provides some fundamental and provocative analyses in response to the question of conservatism.

Sarason (1982) starts with the observation that being a classroom teacher by itself is not a very good preparation for being an effective principal. In their interaction with principals, says Sarason, teachers (as future principals) obtain only a very narrow slice of what it means to be a principal. This narrowness of experience is all the more constrained where the teacher's experience is limited to one or two schools. Next, the newly appointed vice-principal or principal often experiences emphasis on maintenance and stability from his or her teachers. Despite the fact that the principal views his or her role as implying leadership, when resistance to recommendations or ideas for change are encountered, principals often respond in one of two ways. According to Sarason, they "assert authority or withdraw from the fray." (Sarason, 1982:160) This is, no doubt, an oversimplification, but Sarason's overall conclusion is that the narrowness of preparation, and the demands for maintaining or restoring stability, encourage principals to play it safe.

Sarason also claims that many people attribute more constraints to the system than is objectively warranted. These self-imposed conceptions of "the system" overgovern what they do:

> While I do not in any way question that characteristics of the system can and do have interfering effects on an individual's performance ... "the system" is frequently conceived by the individual in a way that obscures, many times unwittingly, the range of possibilities available to

3

> him or her. Too frequently the individual's conception of the system serves as a basis for inaction and rigidity, or as a convenient target onto which one can direct blame for most anything. The principal illustrates this point as well or better than anyone else in the school system. (Sarason, 1982: 164)

Sarason then gives several examples of principals who were using atypical procedures (for example, using older students to work with younger ones) in a school system, while other principals in the same system claimed that the system would not allow it, it was counter to policy, one would be asking for trouble, etc. etc. Sarason suggests that the tendency for principals to anticipate trouble from the system is one of the most frequent and strong obstacles to trying new procedures.

Sarason makes three important observations in his analysis:

> First, the knowledge on the part of the principal that what he or she wants to do may and will encounter frustrating obstacles frequently serves as justification for staying near the lower limits of the scope of the role. Second, the principal's actual knowledge of the characteristics of the system is frequently incomplete and faulty to the degree that his or her conception or picture of what the system will permit or tolerate leads the principal to a passive rather than an active role. Third, and perhaps most important, the range in practices among principals within the same system is sufficiently great as to suggest that the system permits and tolerates passivity and activity, conformity and boldness, dullness and excitement, incompetency and competency. (Sarason, 1982: 171)

I am not suggesting that Sarason has it exactly right. There is no doubt that, especially over the last decade, more emphasis has been placed on broadening teacher leadership (thereby increasing the pool of future principals); principal recruitment that includes more women; criteria that value collaboration and improvement; continuous professional development of school leaders; and the like. Yet, principals as dynamic change agents seem to be still in the minority despite at least twenty years of effort.

The Nonrational World

There is no point in lamenting the fact that the system is unreasonable, and no percentage in waiting around for it to become more reasonable. It won't.

As a bridge to new conceptions for the role of the principal, the concept put forth by Patterson et al (1986), of the nonrational world is particularly useful. The nonrational world is not a nonsensical one. Patterson and his colleagues suggest that organizations in today's society do not follow an orderly logic, but a complex one that is often paradoxical and contradictory, but nevertheless understandable and amenable to influence. They contrast the assumptions of the rational conception with those of a nonrational conception on five dimensions. First, goals: school systems are necessarily guided by multiple and sometimes competing goals. Second, power: power in school systems is distributed throughout the organization. Third, decision-making: decision-making is inevitably a bargaining process to arrive at solutions that satisfy a number of constituencies. Fourth, external environment: the public influences school systems in major ways that are unpredictable. Fifth, teaching process: there are a variety of situationally appropriate ways to teach that are effective.

Patterson and colleagues state their basic position contrasting the rational and nonrational models:

> The central difference between the two models lies in their interpretation of reality. Proponents of the rational model believe that a change in procedures will lead to improvement in educational practice. In short the rational model begins with an "if-then" philosophy. If A happens, then B will logically follow. When reality fails to validate this "if-then" perspective (i.e., when B doesn't happen) the argument shifts to an "if-only" position. If only schools will tighten up rules and regulations, improved discipline will follow. If only teachers are given clear directives, then improved teaching will follow. (Patterson et al, 1986:27)

It is more reasonable, argue Patterson and his colleagues, that actions should be based on a conception of the way the world is. The reality is that educational policies get generated through a mixture of educational and political considerations. It will always be more complicated than we want. The message for the principal, as for others, is that there is no point in lamenting the fact that the system is unreasonable, and no percentage in waiting around for it to become more reasonable. It won't.

We need to move away from the notion of how the principal can become lead implementer of multiple policies and programs. Indeed, the problem is not so much the absence of innovations in schools, but the process of too many ad hoc fragmented reforms that come and go with scant attention to coherence and continuity.

What is needed is to reframe the challenge. What does a reasonable leader do, faced with impossible tasks? In the next section, I start by moving outside the educational literature to get at the answer. It is not that existing educational literature is unhelpful. It seems, however, more fruitful to step back and to start with even more basic ideas, because a new conception of the principal's role is needed.

We need to move away from the notion of how the principal can become lead implementer of multiple policies and programs. What is needed is to reframe the question. What does a reasonable leader do, faced with impossible tasks?

We have, it might be said, come some distance since the days of valuing leaders who "run a tight ship." We have gone through the phases of principal "as administrator" and principal as "instructional leader." We have begun to entertain the concept of principal as transformative leader, or as I have argued elsewhere, principal as moral change agent (Fullan, 1993). There is enormous potential in this new view of the leader, but also great frustration because what it means in practice is not particularly clear. The rest of this book is devoted to tackling the problem of the practical clarity of the new work of school leaders.

Chapter 2

The New Conceptions of the Principalship

Principals as Middle Managers

Entrepreneurs exploit innovation. (Drucker 1985)

Principals are middle managers. As such, they face a classical organizational dilemma. Rapport with teachers is critical as is satisfying those in the hierarchy. The endless supply of new policies, programs and procedures ensures that this dilemma remains active. The expectation that principals should be the leaders in the implementation of changes which they have had no hand in developing and may not understand is especially troublesome.

This situation becomes all the more irritating when the "system" generates a constant stream of fragmented, multiple demands lacking coherence and follow-through. In fact, the job cannot be done on these terms. We need to move to a more basic level through new and more powerful concepts. I do this in three ways. First, I start with a critique of management techniques. The literature abounds with new books on the management for change. It is essential to be exquisitely aware of the fundamental limitation of finding the answer "out there." There is no "silver bullet." Second, the best of the new books contain powerful new concepts and ideas. Once understood, they can form a basis for action. However, their value is deceptive. They sound great, but often don't translate into practical action. They are necessary but not sufficient for practical action. Third, in an effort to move to the level of practical application, I present three case examples of how these new concepts might be used concretely in real situations of change. These concern respectively: the case of advocacy and resistance; the case of whole school reform; and the case of school councils. All in all, the ideas presented generate surprising insights and application, which can take us into new realms of action.

Critique of Management Techniques

Henry Mintzberg (1994) wrote the definitive critique, *The Rise and Fall of Strategic Planning.* He concludes, only half-facetiously, "never adopt a [management] technique by its usual name." Richard Farson (1996) wrote the book, *Management of the Absurd,* observing, "once you find a management technique that works, give it up."

Why did these authors draw such seemingly odd conclusions? Most simply, because they want to stress that there are no "silver bullets," no techniques anywhere that will solve the problem or substitute for the commitments, skills, and messiness of acting in complex environments.

Evans (1996) makes the same point using a different line of analysis. The life cycle for leadership theory he claims is:

1. It begins outside of education, developed by political scientists from studies of gifted historical figures or by management experts from studies of gifted business leaders. (No one would ever think of basing a leadership model on studies of gifted school administrators!)

2. It gains favour in corporate America and comes to be a "hot" concept in management writing.

3. As it nears the apex of its influence, someone decides to apply it to education, even if it has little apparent relevance to schools.

4. It grows hot in educational circles as it begins to cool in the corporate world, where it is showing hitherto unnoticed weakness.

5. It is often misapplied in education, either through slavish rigidity (failing to modify the model to fit schools' unique characteristics) or false clarity (adopting the form of the innovation but not its true substance).

6. Well after it has lost its cachet among business leaders, it lingers on in vestigial form in schools and

schools of education, until its popularity finally sub-
sides there, too.

In today's environments, greater diversity and dynamism make fore-
sight and consensus more and more difficult to achieve. The result
is greater anxiety and stress which, as Stacey (1996) observes, is
handled either by withdrawing from the life of the organization, or
by seeking "the latest comprehensive recipe for organizational success" (p. 7). In situations of uncertainty and conflict we respond
exactly the wrong way with "the rigid injunction that people be more
certain and more consensual. Something they cannot do, of course,
simply because it is all too uncertain and conflictual in the first
place" (p. 7).

The starting point, then, for thinking about and conducting
leadership for change is to be deeply and explicitly aware that there
is no "silver bullet" or set of techniques that can do the job.
Techniques, at best, are tools in the service of a mindset (and associated knowledge and skills), which have been earned through the
hard work of action and reflection, and which are continually honed
through learning on and off the job. Mintzberg's full quote (from
the reference above) captures this orientation nicely:

> Never adopt a technique by its usual name. If you want
> to do re-engineering, or whatever, call it something differ-
> ent so that you have to think it through for yourself and
> work it out on your own terms. If you just adopt it and
> implement it, it is bound to fail. (1994:27)

Put differently, there are no shortcuts. Leaders for change must
immerse themselves in real situations of reform and begin to craft
their own theories of change, constantly testing them against new
situations and the accounts of others' experience.

New Concepts

Peter Block (1987) was one of the first writers to introduce some
of the new concepts for middle management in his *The Empowered
Manager.* Keeping in mind what was just said in the previous section
— don't take any management book as gospel — Block stimulates
new thinking.

Block talks about a quiet revolution in innovative organizations away from tighter controls, precisely defined jobs, and close supervision, and toward the entrepreneurial spirit. This spirit is typified by responsibility, public accountability, interactive professionalism, and the recognition that playing positive politics is essential, possible, and the key to effectiveness. Using the concepts of entrepreneurial spirit and positive political skills, Block builds the case that it is possible for middle managers to shape, if not create, organizations that they believe in, even in the midst of the nonrational world.

Almost as if he were inside the public school system, Block begins by stating: "At the deepest level, the enemy of high performing systems is the feeling of helplessness that so many of us in organizations seem to experience" (p.1). Political skill means making improvements in organizations in a way that maintains and enhances the support of those above and below us. Block cuts right to the fundamental issue early:

> The core of the bureaucratic mindset is not to take responsibility for what is happening. Other people are the problem ... Reawakening the original spirit means we have to confront the issue of our own autonomy. To pursue autonomy in the midst of a dependency-creating culture is an entrepreneurial act. (Block, 1987:6)

Block describes individuals using politics in a traditional, hierarchical organization as becoming good at manipulating other people, managing information to their own advantages, becoming calculating in relationships, and being cautious about telling the truth. He then challenges, "Why get better at a bad game?" We need to get better, says Block, in being positively political "as an act of service, contribution, and creation" (p.9).

The fundamental choices according to Block are between maintenance and greatness, between caution and courage, and between dependency and autonomy. Maintenance includes being preoccupied with playing it safe. It means holding on to what we have and not risking making mistakes. Mistakes are frowned on more than achievements are rewarded. Choosing greatness ups the stakes. Mere improvement is not good enough, says Block.

Related to maintenance is caution: the message of bureaucracies is to be careful. Performance reviews and implementation plans may symbolize the pressure to be careful, even though they frequently are intended to produce the opposite. To confront an issue when others are acting as if there is no issue is an act of courage.

Organizations that say they value autonomy and then look for conformity foster a dependency mentality. Block (1987:15) asserts: "Autonomy is the attitude that my actions are my own choices and the organization I am a part of is in many ways my own creation." He continues:

> We hear people constantly calling for strong leadership. Everyone is waiting for top management to get its act together. When is top management going to give vision and direction to this organization? We focus a great deal on supervisory style and say with certainty that the supervisor sets the tone for how other people behave ...

> All of these wishes for changes above us are examples of our dependency. They all imply that until something above me changes, do not expect me to operate much differently ...

> The price we pay for dependency is our own sense of helplessness. Helplessness and waiting for clear instructions before acting are the opposite of the entrepreneurial spirit ... I must confront my own wish for dependency and move in the direction of autonomy ... (Block, 1987:16-17)

If we move in the direction of autonomy, says Block, we can get on with the business of changing the organization, rather than waiting for direction.

Block concludes his introduction to the topic by acknowledging that there are times when it is necessary to play it safe, such as when we are new on the job and our knowledge is limited; when the organization is under attack and survival is at stake; when we have just gone through considerable risk; and when there is zero trust in the environment. These conditions notwithstanding, the message from Block is that we play it safe far too often, echoing

Sarason's observations, reported earlier, that principals' conceptions of the "system" needlessly limit what they can do. Acting autonomously, and with initiative, has elements of risk, but it is one of the few ways of breaking the cycle. In many circumstances, people find that autonomous action, when tried, is tolerated and even rewarded.

Block summarizes his analysis in these powerful words:

> The key to positive politics, then, is to look at each encounter as an opportunity to support autonomy and to create an organization of our own choosing. It requires viewing ourselves as the primary instrument for changing the culture. Cultures get changed in a thousand small ways, not by dramatic announcements emanating from the boardroom. If we wait until top management gives leadership to the change we want to see, we miss the point. (pp.97-98)

The issue, then, is not the bureaucratic one of how to implement everything that is supposed to be implemented: it is finding one's meaningful place among the multiplicity of choices. Entrepreneurs exploit innovation!

Peter Senge (1990) pushed these new concepts to new levels of insight in *The Fifth Discipline*. He first disposes of the wrong-headed view — still prominent in much of the management literature — that visionary leadership from the top is the answer:

> Our traditional views of leaders — as special people who set the direction, make key decisions, and energize the troops — are deeply rooted in an individualistic and non-systemic world view. Especially in the West, leaders are *heroes* — great men (and occasionally women) who 'rise to the fore' in times of crises. Our prevailing leadership myths are still captured by the captain of the cavalry leading the charge to rescue the settlers from the attacking Indians. So long as such myths prevail, they reinforce a focus on short-term events and charismatic heroes rather than on systemic forces and collective learning. At its heart, the traditional view of leadership is based on assumptions of people's powerlessness, their lack of per-

sonal vision and inability to master the forces of change, deficits which can be remedied only by a few great leaders. (p. 340)

Senge (1990) also put us on the right track in his description of the new work of the leader: as designer, as steward, as teacher. As designers:

> The leaders who fare best are those who continually see themselves as designers not crusaders. Many of the best intentioned efforts to foster new learning disciplines flounder because those leading the charge forget the first rule of learning: people learn what they need to learn, not what someone else thinks they need to learn.

> In essence, the *leader's task is designing the learning processes* whereby people throughout the organization can deal productively with the critical issues they face, and develop their mastery in the learning disciplines. This is new work for most experienced managers, many of whom rose to the top because of their decision-making and problem-solving skills, not their skills in mentoring, coaching, and helping others learn. (p. 345, italics in original)

As stewards, leaders continually seek and oversee the broader purpose and direction of the organization:

> In a learning organization, leaders may start by pursuing their own vision, but as they learn to listen carefully to others' visions, they begin to see that their own personal vision is part of something larger. This does not diminish any leader's sense of responsibility for the vision — if anything it deepens it. (p. 352)

Leader as teacher is not about teaching other people one's own vision:

> Leaders in learning organizations have the ability to conceptualize their strategic insights so that they become public knowledge, open to challenge and further improvement ... [Leader as teacher] is about fostering learning for everyone. Such leaders help people throughout the

organization develop systemic understandings. Accepting this responsibility is the antidote to one of the most common downfalls of otherwise gifted learners — losing their commitment to the truth. (p. 356)

In my own *Change Forces,* eight lessons are identified, derived from the conclusion that change processes these days are inevitably non-linear and chaotic, and that effective leaders are those who are able to foster and/or capitalize on periodic patterns that occur over time. The eight lessons themselves are laced with dilemmas that require leaders to work with opposing tendencies by bringing them into dynamic tension:

Lesson One: You Can't Mandate What Matters
(The more complex the change the less you can force it.)

Lesson Two: Change is a Journey not a Blueprint
(Change is non-linear, loaded with uncertainty, excitement, and sometimes perversity.)

Lesson Three: Problems are Our Friends
(Problems are inevitable and you can't learn without them.)

Lesson Four: Vision and Strategic Planning Come Later
(Premature visions and planning blind.)

Lesson Five: Individualism and Collectivism Must Have Equal Power
(There are no one-sided solutions to isolation and groupthink.)

Lesson Six: Neither Centralization Nor Decentralization Work
(Both top-down and bottom-up strategies are necessary.)

Lesson Seven: Connection with the Wider Environment is Critical for Success
(The best organizations learn externally as well as internally.)

Lesson Eight: Every Person is a Change Agent
(Change is too important to leave to the experts. Personal mindset and mastery are the ultimate protection.)
(Fullan, 1993: 21-22)

Leaders, then, must foster a climate where people are able to work with polar opposites; push for valued change while allowing self-learning to unfold; see problems as sources of creative resolution; have good ideas but not be blinded by them; and strive for internal cohesion as they are externally oriented.

These new ideas have been greatly enhanced by the presence of more women in the role of principalship and by the growing knowledge base related to feminists' conceptions of leadership. Women, more than men, tend to negotiate conflict in ways that try to preserve relationships, to value relationships in and of themselves as part of their commitment to care, and to be socialized in a way that prepares them better to work in collaborative organizations.

The critical ideas, as Henry (1996) observes, include the value of horizontal and inclusionary leadership, the urgent need for relationships of care, the celebration of pluralism and diversity, and the commitment to interacting with communities with empathy and two-way communication (see also Rothschild, 1990). This does not mean that all women teachers will make better principals than men, but it does mean that, in the long-run, our models of the principalship will be substantially strengthened by the growth of forms of collaboration and community-building, represented by this body of research and practice.

The new conceptions of leadership represented in the literature just reviewed call for new work on the part of school leaders. However inspiring as this literature is, I maintain that at the end of the day, it is very difficult for even the committed reader to know what to do. We get the sense that neither the passive, facilitative leader, who tries to be responsive to others, nor the forceful, charismatic leader is effective. The former leader fails to stand for anything, and the latter dominates the agenda. Is there a middle ground? What can school principals do when faced with typical paradoxical solutions? To answer these questions, I provide three practical case illustrations of problems currently facing school principals.

Leadership for Change in Action

The case of advocacy and resistance

The message is to seek and listen to dissent when all your intuition tells you the opposite.

Leaders are urged to foster experimentation, but what if staff appears uninterested in trying new things? Principals are expected to promote some of the latest innovations, but what if staff are not committed to innovation? If we look deeply enough, the new conceptions of leadership give guidance about how to handle these kinds of situations. Gitlin and Margonis (1995) state it this way:

> We believe teachers' initial expressions of cynicism about reform should not automatically be viewed as obstructionist acts to overcome. Instead, time should be spent looking carefully at those resistant acts to see if they might embody a form of good sense — potential insights into the root causes of why the more things change the more they stay the same. (p. 386-387)

Their case study of site-based reform shows how a well-intentioned administrator went about promoting the innovation, working with career ladder teachers, attempting to overcome resistance on the part of teachers. On the surface the principal did most things that the literature on transformational leadership would endorse. For Gitlin and Margonis, there was a failure to get at two root causes: new authority relations where teachers would indeed have more power; and need for examining the structures and availability of time to manage the new demands.

Let's build the case, however, in a more simple manner. Assume that you are a principal who is strongly committed to the increased use of technology. You are sincerely convinced that it is in the best interest of students to become technologically proficient. To keep the example uncomplicated, we must leave aside a number of contextual questions we would have to have answered. We can contrast then, the old and the new way of approaching the situation. By the old, I mean the superficial reading of the literature. By the new, I mean a deeper understanding of leadership for change.

In the old way, your thinking would be like the following: "I am sure that technology is one of the keys to the future for my students; parents support it; I know that some teachers favour it, but others are going to be Luddites. How can I get some teacher leaders to support it? What kind of external resources and expertise can I generate to provide support and pressure to move forward? Maybe I can secure a few transfers and new appointments. My whole approach is advocacy and co-optation into an agenda that I am sure is right."

In the new way, I am equally convinced that technology is critical, but I approach it differently. Cutting the story short, let's say that I am having a staff session in which I am about to show a video segment that portrays a highly successful technology-based school in action. Instead of showing it to make my case, I present it differently. I randomly ask one half of the staff to view the video with a "positive lens," noting what might be in it for us; I ask the other half of the staff to view it "negatively or critically," by identifying what might be problematic or potentially negative for us. If I am sincere, I have legitimized dissent. I have made it easy for staff to speak up about concerns (which would come out later anyway in more subtle and/or inaccessible ways). I listen carefully, suspending my own advocacy, because I know that some fundamental problems will be identified, and that people's fears, real or imagined, will need to be examined carefully. This information may lead me to go back to the drawing board or to work with staff on some preconditions that would have to be addressed, or to proceed into action on a "start small, think big" basis, or to abandon high-profile technology in favour of a different approach.

There is no right answer in this case, but consider the underlying theory. This is what is meant in the new literature by "disagreement is not bad."

> A culture that squashes disagreement is a culture doomed to stagnate, because change always begins with disagreement. Besides disagreement can never be squashed entirely. It gets repressed, to emerge later as a pervasive sense of injustice, followed by apathy, resentment, and even sabotage. (Champy, 1995: 82)

Similarly, Maurer (1996) wrote a whole book on the necessity of embracing, valuing, and seeking new learnings in the energy of resistance; and the corresponding costs of reacting negatively to resistance. Even the army in its new training, emphasizes that "disagreement is not disrespect in the learning organization; it is essential for growth." (Sullivan & Harper, 1996). The message is to seek and listen to dissent, when all your intuition tells you the opposite.

The case of whole school reform

Christensen (1994) conducted a thorough review of the literature on the role of the principal before launching her own investigation into the role of the principal in transforming an "Accelerated School." She portrayed the difference in the literature between the role of the principal in the traditional school versus the restructured school. Our interest here is how the conception in the restructured school stacks up against Christensen's findings in her own study — findings carefully documented through the analysis of over 1000 "critical incidents" of behavior, cross-validated in open-ended questions she asked in the five accelerated schools she studied.

The top behaviors cited in the literature were different in priority compared to those found by Christensen. The literature places "communicates goals," "shares decision-making," "creates/articulates school vision" and "supports staff" (the one overlap) at the top of the list. Christensen found that "fostering the process", "supporting staff", "promoting learning" and "promoting parent involvement" were the major behavior categories with "promote the vision of the school" as an important, but more distant priority (it ranked 10th in frequency out of 13 categories) (Christensen, 1994:113).

We must be careful not to misinterpret these findings. They do not say, for example, that creating a vision is unimportant. But they do put it in perspective, showing that it is subordinate in some ways to a more sophisticated process. Second, although we do not have the specifics here, it is crucial that leaders understand the discrete behaviors that made up the categories. For example, "use the governance process correctly" was one of 18 subcategories of "fostering the process" and itself had a dozen types of critical incidents of behavior such as:

- don't make administrative mandates that affect the whole school without going through the process;

- make sure decisions are not made in a hurry;

- don't take over meetings; be a co-participant;

- get input from all stakeholders; and

- encourage consensus rather than voting. (Ibid, p.120)

Similarly, in interviews, the top "things a principal must do to be a good accelerated school principal" according to principals and teachers were:

- be willing to let go of control;

- be supportive of staff;

- be present;

- stand up to the district;

- be a real expert on the accelerated school process;

- be positive;

- believe every child is a success;

- be open-minded; listen to everybody's opinions; and

- be sensitive to staff morale. (Ibid, p. 132)

It is obviously not helpful to try and memorize the list of behaviors, but a pattern is emerging. Effective principals extend as well as express what they value. They nurture a subtle process of enabling teachers to work together to generate solutions. It is easy for principals with good ideas to let themselves get seduced into "taking over." Prestine's (1994) study of a "Coalition of Essential Schools" reform that got bogged down, but eventually regrouped, illustrates this problem clearly.

When progress was faltering, the principal became more and more concerned:

Taking charge of the meetings, the principal assigned a series of discrete tasks, built around authentic assessment ideas, to be completed by faculty groups. In essence, nothing happened. As the principal noted, "I gave an assignment. I can't believe I tried this. No one read the book. No one understood what I was talking about. It was like I was talking Swahili. The whole thing sort of fell flat. (Prestine, 1994: 134)

Reflecting on this the principal observed:

I allowed the faculty to push responsibility for their learning onto me. Even worse, I went out and provided the venue in which it would happen. I did something I swore I would never do — take responsibility for a school's behavior, for the learning of individual teachers. I took direct managerial responsibilities. Worse yet, the model I set up was exactly the kind of instruction I had never done as a teacher — that is, I give you an assignment and you do exactly as I told you to do. It was terrible as I came to understand what I had been doing. (Ibid, p. 135)

As one of the teacher co-ordinators observed:

We suddenly realized what was wrong. We realized that we did not have ownership anymore ... He [the principal] seemed to know everything there was to know about it, so it was necessary to push it onto him. Once we did that, it was doomed to failure. (Ibid, p. 135)

The point here is not that these mistakes can be eliminated. Rather, you need enough of a working theory of leadership for change, combined with mechanisms for personal and collective reflection, so that you inevitably self-correct, thereby deepening the internalization of theory and your capacity to act effectively the next time, and the time after that, and so on.

These developments are part and parcel of a more fundamental change in the culture of schools, which we take up in some depth in our companion volume, *What's Worth Fighting For? Working Together For Your School*. Leaders and learning organizations know that *both* individualism and collaboration must co-exist. They know that isolation is bad, but that collaboration has downsides too — not the least of which are balkanization and groupthink. They know that differences, diversity and conflict are not only inevitable, but that they often contain the seeds of breakthrough. Homogenous cultures are more peaceful, but they are also more stagnant than heterogeneous cultures.

The case of School Councils

Nothing motivates a child more than when learning is valued by school, family, and community working in partnership.

The establishment of school councils with parent and community participation in advisory or decision making roles is an international phenomenon of major proportions. What is the principal as change agent to make of these developments? The old way of responding would be to treat it as a necessary evil — something to be tolerated, blunted — or to go about dutifully trying to make the council work. Both of these responses are narrow and limiting as a broader conception and considerable evidence reveals.

The principal steeped in leadership for change would have a different approach. First, he or she would recognize the emergence of school councils as part of a systemic shift in the relationship between the communities and schools that is both inevitable and that contains the seeds of a necessary realignment with the family and other social agencies. Put another way, the principal would not take school councils literally, but would see them as the tip of a more complex and powerful iceberg. Systemic thinking says that boundaries need to be more permeable and that greater interaction across systems is essential to long-term success.

Second, and to be much more specific, research and best practice are abundantly clear: Nothing motivates a child more than when learning is valued by school, family, and community working in partnership. Furthermore, you can do something to improve this relationship through deliberate action. For the same reason that site-based management (involving teachers) bears no relationship to changes in the culture and learning of the whole school, the presence of school councils per se does not affect student learning. The establishment of a council involving a handful of parents could not possibly improve the learning for the hundreds of students in the school (see Wylie's (1995) assessment of the New Zealand experience). What does make a difference is the multiple forms of particular involvement deliberately fostered, developed and supported. Programs which increase the capacity of parents and schools to partner are needed. (Epstein, 1995)

Third, in thinking and working through these developments, the principal's theory of change becomes much more powerful. It becomes clearer in what Sarason (1995) and Ontario's Royal Commission on Learning (1994) meant when they said that school councils or parent involvement is not an end in itself. Shifts in power are involved, but it is not power in and of itself that counts, but what the new power arrangement can actually do:

> To seek power is to raise and begin to answer the question: to seek power to change *what*? Changing the forces of power in no way guarantees that anything else will change ... To seek power without asking the "what" question is not only to beg the question but to avoid it and, therefore, to collude in cosmetic changes. (Sarason, 1995:53, his emphasis)

Dolan draws this powerful conclusion:

> To educate children without a deep partnership of teacher and parent is hopeless, and going in we have conditioned everyone to minimal interaction, indifference, maybe even suspicion. This is the (Steady State) in most of the country. And, it has to change. (p. 159)

Fourth, and once again we see the operational principles of leadership for change in action, ideas about diversity and conflict become a natural part of the creation of something new:

> In a school, where mistrust between the community and the administration is the major issue, you might begin to deal with it by making sure that parents were present at every major event, every meeting, every challenge. *Within the discomfort of that presence*, the learning and the healing could begin. (Dolan, 1994: 60, my emphasis)

Similarly, without knowledge for change, school councils can easily become diversions where energy is diverted to compliance and power struggles not to capacity building. A school council, as surprising as this may seem:

> ... is *not* primarily a decision-making mechanism. This is not principalship by committee. A Site Council that focusses only on decision-making tends to make the intervention solely a power issue. It often exhausts itself on petty issues and control struggles and never gets to the main business which is *driving* the change. (Dolan, 1994: 131, his emphases)

Rather, the role of the council is to help mobilize the forces and resources for change by developing the skills of parents, teachers, students and principals as leaders in "group problem-solving," "dealing with conflict," and "making content expertise accessible." (Ibid. p. 134) This brings new, more complex meaning to the role of the principal in the middle.

School councils are but one of the many new forms or reframing relationships with an environment that has become more intrusive and boundaries that are increasingly transparent — a theme we take up in depth in *What's Worth Fighting For Out There?* (Hargreaves and Fullan, *forthcoming*).

All three case examples in this section are powerful reminders of how fundamentally the role requirements of school principals have changed. There is greater internal and external complexity; there is greater need for building relationships in situations of diversity and conflict; there is more need for fighting against systems that foster dependency and otherwise keep the principal off balance; there is more call for reflection and proaction. In this new world, principals have much that is worth fighting for — for those they serve, but also for their own good as moral change agents.

In this new world, principals have much that's worth fighting for.

Chapter 3

Guidelines for Action

The starting point for what's worth fighting for is not system change, not change in others around us, but change in ourselves.

To be practical, two areas of action are required simultaneously. First, in the short and continuing long run, a higher proportion of incumbent principals must take charge. The question of what's worth fighting for must be addressed and acted upon immediately — today, tomorrow, next week. Second, and in the mid-run, school systems must take action to create, insist on, support and be responsive to the conditions for school-based action — not in isolation, but as part of a visible, interactive network of public commitment to actual and acknowledged improvement.

What's Worth Fighting For?

Block (1987) tells the story of consulting with a large supermarket chain in the United States in which one of the main goals was to shift decision-making to the level of store managers, much as some school systems have attempted to move toward greater school-based decision-making. The company had done a number of things (role clarification, training, communication meetings, and so forth) to try to shift power to the store manager and experienced little success. In assessing the situation, the common complaint was that the chain could not expect store managers to change their role without active day-to-day support of the district managers, whose role is comparable to that of education's area superintendents. Work with district managers was incorporated, but it too failed to make much of a difference. At that point, divisional managers, much like education's central office superintendents, were cited as creating or being a possible barrier. Division managers received attention with still only small improvements. A meeting was then scheduled with the President who might be compared to an education Director. While he had endorsed all the efforts to change, it was felt that perhaps he as well, should be the target of change. His complaint was that he too was in the middle, because he found it difficult to please those above him who could be compared to a Board of Education because he felt helpless to influence on any scale, those below him. When all was said and done years of organizational development efforts across the different levels resulted in very slow movement toward the goal.

The point of the supermarket story is not that some organizations are better than others, or that everything is related to everything else. The story illustrates four very important issues related to our pursuit.

1. There is a tendency to externalize the problem, and to look for blockages at other levels of the system. Whether this is true or not in a given situation is irrelevant to the main point: waiting for others to act differently results in inaction and playing it safe.

2. There is an assumption that the entire "system" must be changed before improvements will occur — a chicken and egg stance which also immobilizes people.

3. Almost everyone perceives themselves to be in the "middle" in some way, in the sense that there are people above them expecting more, and people below them who are immune to influence.

4. Everyone has some power, most often used *not* to do things.

All of this is to say that the starting point for what's worth fighting for is not system change, not change in others around us, but change in ourselves. This is both more achievable and paradoxically is the first step toward system change because it contributes actions not words.

Ten guidelines for individual action can be suggested. It is essential that these guidelines be viewed in concert, not as actions isolated from one another.

1. Avoid "if only" statements, externalizing the blame and other forms of wishful thinking.

2. Start small, think big. Don't overplan or overmanage.

3. Focus on fundamentals: curriculum, instruction, assessment, professional culture.

4. Practice fearlessness and other forms of risk taking.

5. Embrace diversity and resistance while empowering others.

6. Build a vision in relation to both goals and change processes.

7. Decide what you are *not* going to do.

8. Build allies.

9. Know when to be cautious.

10. Give up the search for the "silver bullet."

Guidelines for Principals

1. Avoid "if only ..." statements

In most cases, "if only" statements beg the question, externalize the blame, and immobilize people. "If only" the superintendents were better leaders; "if only" the Board would allocate more resources to professional development; "if only" the State or Provincial Department of Education would stop issuing so many policy changes and so forth. All of these wishes for changes around us, according to Block, are expressions of dependency and foster a sense of helplessness. As Block sums it up, "waiting for clear instructions before acting is the opposite of the entrepreneurial spirit." (p. 16) Another way of putting it is, "What can I do that is important to me and those around me?" Guideline one, then, stresses the necessity for moving concretely in the direction of autonomy. In the first instance, what's worth fighting for is more of an internal battle than an external one.

2. Start small, think big. Don't overplan and overmanage

Striving for complexity in the absence of action can generate more clutter than clarity.

Complex changes, (and managing multiple innovations in schools does represent complexity), means facing a paradox. On the one hand, the greater the complexity, the greater the need to address implementation planning; on the other hand, the greater the thoroughness of implementation planning, the more complex the change process becomes. I talk later (in item 3) about what to focus on and (in item 6) about the need for a vision of the change process, but at this point, it seems necessary to caution against overplanning and overmanaging. After a certain amount of goal and priority setting, it is important not to get bogged down in elaborate needs assessment, discussion of goals and the like. Striving for complexity in the absence of action can generate more clutter than clarity. Effective managers have the capacity to short circuit potentially endless discussion and wheel-spinning by getting to the action.

Evidence in both business and education indicates that effective leaders have "a bias for action." They have an overall sense of direction, and start into action as soon as possible, establishing small scale examples, adapting, refining, improving quality, expanding, reshaping as the process unfolds. This strategy might be summed up as "start small: think big," or the way to get better at implementation planning is more by doing than by planning. Ownership is something that is developed through the process rather than in advance. Opportunities for reflection and problem solving are as important during the process as they are before it begins. In this sense, innovations are not things "to be implemented," but are catalysts, points of departure or vehicles for examining the school and for making improvements. "Ready, fire, aim" is a more apt metaphor for capturing the dynamics of nonlinear reform (Fullan, 1993).

For complex changes, tighter forms of planning and managing lose on two counts. They place the principal in a dependent role, however unintended, and they hamper the extension of autonomy to others. Shared control over implementation at the school level is essential.

3.   Focus on fundamentals: curriculum, instruction, assessment, professional culture

Consistency in schools must be obtained at the receiving end not the delivery end.

Here we become involved in setting priorities and in questions of consistency. Priorities are generated through a mixture of political and educational merit. The result, as we have seen, is overload. The best way for a principal to approach situations of impossible overload is to take the stance that "we are going to implement a few things especially well, and implement other priorities as well as we would have anyway, which is to keep them from getting out of hand. We will look for ways of integrating or aligning components that might otherwise be fragmented."

Thus, there is not a call for any new neglect. This guideline assumes that within the array of policy priorities, there are "some things" which can productively be examined and improved. It takes policies not as all things to be implemented, but as some things to be exploited. What's worth fighting for is to select one area or a few instructional areas of major interest and/or need, and intensely pursue them through implementation. For example, a serious attack on an important curriculum area for the school represents a strike for something that is close to the core educational goals of schools even if all potential priorities are not being addressed. Such a positive initiative can be pointed to as an example of commitment and accomplishment in spite of the overload that surrounds schools.

Moreover, there is much greater choice in what can be done than is normally acknowledged. In terms of ends, there are many policy priorities from which one can chose to emphasize. Within selected priority directions, the means of implementation can vary widely. For most policies it is more accurate to treat policy implementation as an opportunity to define and develop the policy further, than it is to conceive of it as putting into practice someone else's ideas. Principals, in effect, have enormous leeway in practice.

Consistency provides sustenance for setting priorities. The combination of overload and frequent, seeming shifts in policy results is de facto eclecticism. Consistency in schools must be obtained at the receiving end not the delivery end. Learning accrues in a school whose staff have "a constructed, continuous shared reality." Learning power comes from the consistent messages that students get about what it is to be an independent learner ... a problem solver ... a reader ... a writer, and so forth. Conversely, schools that are eclectic in their approaches to learning (and the "system" makes it easy to be eclectic) do poorly in terms of independent learning behaviors and achievement. It makes a lot of sense when you think about it, that if the expectations are changed every year then strong, successful learning is not going to accrue.

In addition to concrete curriculum projects, the principal must pay attention to the professional culture of the school focussing on the interrelationship among curriculum, instruction, and assessment, through fostering a professional learning community. Much of this evidence and associated action guidelines are examined in our *What's Worth Fighting For? Working Together For Your School.* We know that professional cultures, with their openness to new ideas, their focus on what and how students are learning, their giving and receiving help, are strongly related to success in continuous improvement. Such collaborative work cultures foster greater coherence and consistency through their constant interaction and focus on what they are doing and on how well they are doing.

Newmann and Wehlage's (1995) study of over 800 schools engaged in restructuring is the latest of many research projects that demonstrate that "school-wide teacher professional community affected the ... classroom pedagogy, which in turn affected student performance" (p. 32). Establishing such collaborative work, depends on effective school leaders who "can make a big difference through hiring, staff development, and establishing a supportive climate" (p. 37). Schools with strong professional communities "pursued a continuous cycle of innovation, feedback, and redesign in curriculum, instruction and assessment" (p. 38).

What's worth fighting for, then, includes fostering collaborative work cultures which create a generic capacity to manage change on a continuous basis.

4. Practise fearlessness

Sarason (1982) described how some principals were carrying out certain practices at the same time that other principals in the same system were saying it was not allowed. How do they get away with it? It is somewhat superficial to say, but nonetheless true, that "they just do it."

Block (1987:178) claims that many people take "safe paths" in complex situations, such as believing simply in rationality, imitating others, or following the rules. He puts forward the idea that improvements are made through "facing organizational realities" by "continual acts of courage." He suggests that if one is guided by vision-building, as outlined in item 6, three "acts" are necessary: (1) "facing the harsh reality," (2) examining "our own contribution to the problem" and (3) making "authentic statements in the face of disapproval."

The tough version of "acts of courage" entails acting on something important, in such a way that we are "almost indifferent to the consequences it might have for us." (p.182) Like most risk-taking, we have to be prepared to lose before we can win. Paradoxically, effective principals, as the research literature indicates, are men and women who take independent stances on matters of importance, and in most cases, are all the more respected for it. At a less dramatic level, I would suggest that fearlessness can be practised on a more modest scale. One need not start by publicly defying the superintendent! Three criteria for beginning might be to be selective, to do it on a small scale and to make a positive rather than a negative act of courage. So, for example, one might make it clear that the latest curriculum directive cannot be immediately addressed because the staff are in the midst of implementing another important priority. Then, the principal can demonstrate willingness to discuss the importance and progress of this other priority. Another example might be presenting a well worked-out plan, asking for modest resources to implement something important to the school and the community.

There is such a thing as occupational suicide and no doubt there are many courageous acts that could be classified as foolish. But given the cautionary tendencies described in earlier sections, it seems legitimate to suggest that an increase in selective acts of fearlessness in reference to a major school goal would be a good thing.

5.   Embrace diversity and resistance while empowering others

Empowerment acts as a safeguard against being wrong and is essential for implementing serious improvements. Empowering others in the school has to form a major component of the effective principal's agenda. It is becoming clearer in the research literature that complex changes in education sometimes require active (top-down or external) initiation, but if they are to go anywhere, there must be a good deal of shared control and decision making during implementation.

From their current research, Miles (1987) and others analyze the successful evolution of effective secondary school programs. In addition to several other factors, many of which are related to other items on our list, Miles stresses that while initiative often comes from the principal, "power sharing" is critical from that point onward. Successful schools were characterized by principals who supported and stimulated initiative-taking by others, who set up cross-hierarchical steering groups consisting of teachers, administrators, and sometimes parents and students, and who delegated authority and resources to the steering group, while maintaining active involvement in or liaison with the groups.

Three other points should be added to the concept of interactive power sharing within the school. First, this is not an individualistic exercise. It is a matter of creating groups responsible for and working on significant tasks. Such peer and hierarchical groups function to integrate both pressure and support to get things done. As it turns out, peer interaction represents a far more powerful form of pressure than traditional hierarchical forms because it combines support and pressure to get things done.

Second, empowerment means additional resources, such as time, money, and personnel. The principal must be able to deliver resources. Sometimes, but not always, he or she does this with extra money. Most times, it is done by helping to invent imaginative ways for freeing up time. Effective principals do the latter all the time, and in ways which other principals either would not think of, or would say could not be done. Another finding of the research is that a little bit of time and resources available regularly can go a long way.

Third, developing a new mindset about the roles of diversity, conflict and resistance is absolutely crucial. Homogenous cultures by definition have less diversity, but they are also more boring. Heterogeneous cultures contain the seeds of creative breakthrough. In addition to collaborative skills, conflict management skills are essential in diverse societies. Conflict is not just a nuisance; it is positively necessary in working out new productive solutions. It is when conflict is mishandled or avoided that it becomes most destructive.

I have already illustrated in the case examples in Chapter Two that differences of opinion and "resistance" must be reframed as *inevitable and desirable* forces of change. Failure to listen to and appreciate points of view different from one's own actually increases resistance, creates fear and suspicion, and separates us from others. The alternative, albeit counterintuitive, is to "embrace resistance, respect those who resist, and join with the resistance" to listen, understand and find common ground for new possibilities. (Maurer, 1996:54)

It is possible, indeed essential, to understand that this does not mean simply going with the flow. In *What's Worth Fighting For? Working Together For Your School,* we advised principals "to express what they value," as well as "to extend what they value." Having good ideas and strong images of the future means, in the words of Maurer, that one must "maintain a clear focus" over the long run. It is the combination of moral purpose, valuing diversity, listening and learning, persistence and intermittent consolidation through shared synergy, that makes the difference.

6. Build a vision relevant to both goals and processes

An organization, to be effective, needs both a vision of the nature or content that it represents, and a clear vision of the processes it characteristically values and follows.

Vision-building feeds into and is fed by all other guidelines in this section. It cuts through the tendency to blame others; it provides a sense of direction for starting small but thinking big; it provides focus; it checks random fearlessness; it gives content to empowerment and alliance discussions; it gives direction for deciding what not to do; it eschews easy solutions. Above all, it permeates the enterprise with values, purpose, and informs both the "what" and the "how" of improvement.

Block provides examples of guiding beliefs or visions: we act as partners with our customers; we choose quality over speed; we want to understand the impact of our actions on our customers; we want consistency between our plans and action; we value high standards and expectations in our board; we support the decentralization of decisions as close to the point of implementation as possible; and so on. These basic values guide specific priorities (such as, every child in this school will concentrate on good writing) and are translated into consistent day to day actions over time.

The vital role of vision appears in every book on educational and organizational excellence. It is not an easy concept with which to work, and I have cautioned elsewhere to avoid short cuts and premature visions that have no depth or communal meaning (Fullan, 1993). An organization, to be effective, needs both a vision of the nature or content that it represents, and a clear vision of the processes it characteristically values and follows. Vision is not something that someone happens to have; it is a much more fluid process and does not have to be — indeed it must not be — confined to a privileged few. In a real sense, implementation of any policy will be superficial unless all implementers come to have a deeply held version of the meaning and the importance of the change for them.

To start with the leader, Bennis and Nanus (1988) make it quite clear that top leaders in their study had, but did not invent, visions for their organizations. Indeed, these leaders were more likely to be good at extracting and synthesizing images from a variety of sources:

> All of the leaders to whom we spoke seemed to have been masters at selecting, synthesizing, and articulating an appropriate vision of the future ... If there is a spark of genius in the leadership function at all, it must lie in this transcending ability, a kind of magic, to assemble — out of all the variety of images, signals, forecasts and alternatives — a clearly articulated vision of the future that is at once single, easily understood, clearly desirable, and energizing. (p.101)

Vision must be something arguably of value. It should be somewhat lofty or uplifting. It should have some concreteness. Block emphasizes that "creating a vision forces us to take a stand for a preferred future." (1987:102) Vision also must withstand the marketplace, and therefore has to make a contribution to what is important for significant others. Focussing on the clients, parents and children, and connecting with others in the organization to formulate an image of what we want for the future, begins the process of transcending the present.

We normally think of vision as something in the future, but we do not necessarily think in terms of how to get to that vision. When we do address the "how," it is often formulated in a top-down manner — form a task force, clarify the vision, communicate and train it, assess it, etc. etc. As we now turn more directly to the aspects of process, a number of other dimensions must be introduced. Working on one's own vision is the starting point. The extension of this position is that it is the task of each person in the organization, to a certain extent, to create their own version of the vision of the future. Obviously, interactive professionalism and collaborative cultures will result in commonalities. Visions will tend to converge, if the guidelines in this section are followed. This will sometimes result in sharper differences, but the more serious problem seems to be the absence of clearly articulated visions rather than a multiplicity of them.

The dialogue about vision, according to Block, should strive to achieve three qualities: depth, clarity, and responsibility relative to the vision. Depth is the degree to which the vision statement is personally held. Clarity comes from insisting on specific images. Vagueness, says Block, "is a way of not making a commitment to a vision." (p. 124). Responsibility involves moving from helplessness to active ownership: " ... the primary reason we demand that people create a vision statement is to reinforce the belief that all of us are engaged in the process of creating this organization." (p. 124)

It cannot be overemphasized that this guideline incorporates commitment to both the content of vision and to the *process* of vision-building and implementation. It is in fact a dynamic and fluid relationship in which the vision of the school is shaped and reshaped as people try to bring about improvements. It is a difficult balance, but commitment and skill in the change process on the part of organizational leaders and members is every bit as crucial as ideas about where the school should be heading.

The continuous process of vision-building in an organization requires a number of skills and qualities. Two-way communication skills, risk-taking, the balancing of clarity and openness, the combining of pressure and support, integrity, positive regard for others, and a perpetual learning orientation, all figure in the dynamic process of developing a shared vision in the school. In Miles' (1987) terms, the process involves issues of *will* (such as risk-taking and tolerance of uncertainty) and *skill* (such as organizational design, the support of others, clear communication, the development of ownership). The shared vision, in short, is about the content of the school as it might become, and the nature of the change process that will get us there.

Consider the result of shared vision-building. You and others in the school become the resident experts. You know what you are doing. You know more about the program than any outsider. You can demonstrate and explain the program. You are in a better position to deflect unwanted demands because you can point to something substantial. You have critical criteria to serve as a screening mechanism for sorting out which demands to act on seriously and which opportunities to seek. You are, in a word, in a better position to act fearlessly.

7.   Decide what you are not going to do

The principal's job is to ensure that essential things get done, not to do them all himself or herself.

If the principal tries to do everything that is expected, he or she expends incredible energy with little or nothing to show for it. Therefore, one of the most neglected aspects of what's worth fighting for is how to say "no" and yet maintain, indeed enhance, one's reputation and the respect others have for that individual.

There are two features of principals' work which present them with aggravation. One is the endless stream of meetings and new policy and program directives, already described. The other is a daily schedule which consists of continual interruptions. There are plenty of studies of the individual work days of principals, and they draw the same conclusions: principals' work days are characterized by dozens of small interactions. The research literature has come to label the work of principals as involving brevity, variety, and fragmentation.

Principals, above all, are "victims of the moment." Because of the immediacy and physical presence of interruptions, principals are constantly dragged into the crises of the moment. These include telephone calls, two students fighting, salespeople, parents wanting to see them, calls from central office to check into something or to come to an urgent meeting, etc. etc.

Dependency on the moment is not inevitable, however. Four strategies for maintaining initiative and control are: maintaining focus, making your position clear to the superintendent, managing time accordingly and saying no.

Vision-building is central to selecting and maintaining focus. To simplify the matter, two issues are of first order of importance; instructional leadership and public relations. Instructional leadership means working with teachers and others to decide on the most important needs of the school, whether it be English as a Second Language, language and writing across the curriculum, primary/junior science, or whatever. Responsiveness to the community is part and parcel of needs assessment and maintaining focus. Consent, and in some cases, involvement of parents, are essential. The priority, in relation to the community, is instructionally-focussed public relations, not random communication.

Making one's position clear to the first line superintendent is ideally an interactive process. The emphasis should be on the principal taking charge. The principal, in effect, is saying to the superintendent that instructional leadership is his or her number one priority. The particular priorities arrived at may be done in full cooperation with the superintendent or in a more distant manner; in either case, the principal makes it a point that the superintendent understands the priority and the flow of actions being taken. The basic message is that if there is an instructional activity in his or her school, and there is a meeting which conflicts, he or she cannot attend the meeting but will send someone else. This is not a matter of being stubborn or rigid. Without such protection, a principal's time would get totally eaten up by unconnected activities which amount to nothing. By explaining one's position in terms of specific instructional activities, it turns out that very few meetings are so important that they cannot be missed. Many superintendents would value such a focus and stance, but let me say some would not. This is where selective fearlessness comes in. A little assertiveness in the service of a good cause where you have teacher and community backing may be necessary. There is nothing wrong with saying "no."

Managing time is related to both attitude and technique. Protecting priority time, sometimes fiercely, is a must. Staying focussed might mean, for example, setting aside a morning to plan a professional growth session for staff, and then sticking to it. It can be made clear that "nobody is to interrupt" during that time. Exceptions may occur in extreme situations, but telephone calls, even aggressive ones, can be handled by a secretary, delayed or scheduled in.

A second aspect of managing time is how to handle central office events. A principal might make a choice not to attend meetings which are purely informational. Acting as a filter for unproductive requests is another important component. If the principal tries to respond to all central office requests, the school will get pulled in too many different directions. If the meeting is truly important, the principal can attend or send someone else who may be more centrally involved with the item being addressed. I will not reiterate the earlier discussion that the principal has no choice if the superintendent is doing the requesting. There is an element of risk-taking, but not as much as is assumed when positive instructional focusses are what drive the principal.

Delegation, the third aspect of time management, is an orientation and skill that only a minority of middle managers have mastered. It amounts to the advice to try not to do anything that someone else in the building can do, because principals need to spend their time on what others in the building are not in a position to do. For example, why should a principal plan track and field days when teachers can do it better because it is for their students? Why should a principal collect and count trip money? Why should a principal fill out straightforward statistical reports, do the paperwork for teacher absence, and the like? Training office staff is a related and much undeveloped skill. Delegation does not mean absence of communication. The principal's job is to ensure that essential things get done, not to do them all himself or herself.

Saying "no" is a summation of the advice of this guideline. Principals spend too much time on things that are not essential. There are few things that absolutely must be done, cannot be delayed or cannot be delegated. Only a small proportion of what principals do is apparently centrally related to instruction. Diversions, of course, also plague principals who have an instructional focus. But, they have learned to say "no." Otherwise, the whole day would be spent running around with nothing to show for the effort except stress and with no sense of accomplishment other than short term survival. Principals must get more in the habit of saying "no," or of rescheduling things for a time when they can be addressed more efficiently. I stress, as I did at the outset, that this is not a matter of letting the principal "off the hook" under the guise of autonomy. The focussed, interactive, interdependent principal is a socially responsible being, working avidly on the improvement of the school. The effective principal is more public than private. Without question, however, what's worth fighting for is saying "no" to tasks and activities that do not contribute, in a sustained way, to the betterment of the school.

The focussed, interactive, interdependent principal is a socially responsible being, working avidly on the improvement of the school.

8. Build allies

It is foolhardy to continue to act fearlessly if you are not at the same time developing alliances. One of the most encouraging developments over the last decade is the presence of more and more potential allies who seem to want to support and move in the direction of greater school-based implementation. Criteria for promotion tend more and more to emphasize curricular leadership, capacity for working effectively with others and ability to lead interactive forms of development whether they involve coaching, performance appraisal or curriculum implementation.

With this potential, the principal should seek alliances, through specific projects and activities, with at least five groups — senior level administrators, peers, parents, teachers, and individuals who

39

are external to the system (in the Ministry of Education and Training, faculties of education, innovative networks, and so forth).

Peers — other principals and vice-principals — can also be significant sources of support in the short and long run. It may require some initiative and risk-taking, but principals who go out of their way to work cooperatively with other principals on a curriculum project, and who share information and resources, develop both a reputation and a set of relationships which serve them well at points of critical decision.

Alliances with parents are much more tricky. One runs the risk of getting involved with splinter groups and/or offending important political forces on the board. Sticking with valued curriculum priorities can be one safeguard, because work with the community is intended not to block something, but to implement something considered to be valuable. We also saw in our school council case example earlier that there is now a much greater knowledge base for working with parents and communities. The complexities of doing these require school leadership that embodies the kinds of guidelines expressed in this chapter.

Guideline 5 listed earlier stressed empowerment. Such empowerment is reciprocal. Teachers, for example, already have and exercise power *not* to do things. Building a trusted, empowered relationship with teachers usually means that the principal can count on teachers to help implement policies that the principal holds to be important. This relationship puts the principal in a position to be responsive to ideas coming from teachers.

There are, of course, skills involved in negotiating relationships across the groups just described. Block (1987) talks about the critical skills of negotiating agreement and trust. He complicates the matter, realistically, by noting that such negotiations must be undertaken with both allies and adversaries. He outlines a number of steps for dealing with each of the following situations: high agreement/high trust (allies), high trust/low agreement (opponents), high agreement/low trust (bedfellows), low trust/unknown agreement (fence sitters), and low agreement/low trust (adversaries).

This is not the place to delve into these issues, but two conclusions may be made. First, at least some allies in each of the five groups should and can be established. In addition to power bases, such a network serves as a source of ideas, critical feedback, and the like. Second, as Block states: "... people become adversaries only when our attempts at negotiating agreement and negotiating trust have failed" (1987: 144). Our *What's Worth Fighting For Out There? (forthcoming)* contains many additional ideas for building productive alliances with diverse groups in the environment.

9.   Know when to be cautious

Since people exert so much caution naturally, this section can be brief. Block mentioned four circumstances which dictate caution: when we don't know the situation, when survival is at stake, when we are in times following periods of risk and expansion, and when we are in a zero trust environment. (1987: 17-18) Risks can also be reduced by starting small (and thinking big), and trying out ideas on a small scale initially and/or with smaller numbers of people. However, if we are experiencing states of continuous, ever-increasing caution, that is a sign that either we ourselves should change, or move elsewhere to a less repressive organization.

10.   Give up the search for the "silver bullet"

Earlier I criticized the tendency to seek solutions in the latest management techniques, not because the latter are useless, but because there are no shortcuts or panaceas. Management techniques do not have a good track record in business either. They come and go like so many fads, leaving little residue except for false hopes. It could not be otherwise. The complexities of postmodern environments are not amenable to single solutions.

Once we realize that there is no answer, that we will never arrive in any final sense, it can be quite liberating. Instead of hoping that a new technique will at last provide the answer, we approach it differently. Leaders for change get involved as learners in real situations of reform. They craft their own theories of change, constantly testing them against new situations. They become critical consumers of management techniques, able to sort out promising from empty ideas. They become less vulnerable to and less dependent on external solutions. They stop looking for solutions in the wrong places.

Guidelines for School Systems

Err on the side of autonomy over dependency.

This publication is for and about principals, so that the advice for school systems will not be elaborate. Clearly, risk-taking in principals will be inhibited if it is not also a characteristic of superintendents. This is so in two ways. Senior level managers who engage in focussed risk-taking both provide good role models, and create the conditions of pressure and responsiveness for school-level leaders to act similarly.

There are four guidelines which I would highlight:

1. Cherish empowered managers when you find them;

2. Understand the paradoxically simultaneous "loose-tight" relationship between schools and school systems;

3. Concentrate on, and make visible, selection criteria;

4. Establish short- and long-range leadership development plans to produce "willed and skilled" school leaders.

The first guideline is straightforward — err on the side of autonomy over dependency. Superintendents should value, indeed should cherish, the independent, initiative-taking principal who has energized the staff and the community into working on an instructional issue of importance. Superintendents should do this even when they might not fully agree with the particular priority. Empowered principals are not closed-minded, just focussed. Openness is maintained through the highly interactive process described in Chapter Two. Put another way, the principal's priorities are shaped and reshaped through interaction with teachers, parents, consultants and superintendents. The superintendent can be more influential in this kind of relationship than in a more traditional one, because the latter relationship generates superficial conformity at best and resistance at worse, while the former results in action.

Second, understand, conceptualize, and reinforce the paradoxical "tight-loose" relationships required for modern organizations to be effective. It is not a choice between a "top-down" system and isolated autonomy. Just as the principal must foster autonomy and empowerment of teachers, so the central office must do the same in relation to schools. Generally, this means decentralizing decision-making within a framework of priorities, on the one hand. It means staying in close contact throughout the process, which involves approving plans, coordinating resources, facilitating networking, reviewing progress and discussing procedures and policies, on the other hand.

Louis (1987) captures this essence of the necessarily delicate balancing act in her discussion of "loose-tight" district management, in a study of effective secondary schools. She makes the helpful distinction between "coupling" and "bureaucracy," arguing that they are two different dimensions of the relationship:

> By coupling I mean a relationship which has some shared goals and objectives, reasonably clear and frequent communication, and mutual coordination and influence. By bureaucracy I mean control through rules and regulations. (Louis, 1987:161)

Drawing on case studies, Louis describes typical and ineffective school districts as evidencing highly bureaucratic but largely decoupled systems. Says Louis, "in a decoupled but regulatory system the district/school system becomes nothing but an irritating set of constraints and conflicting demands." (p. 24) Strongly-coupled, regulatory, or rule-based systems, fared no better, and were characterized by mistrust on both sides. By contrast, Louis found that "the only clearly positive district contexts are found in cases ... which are *tightly coupled and non-regulatory* ... Essentially, the picture is one of co-management, with coordination and joint planning ..." (p. 25-26). Our own discussion of school level-central level co-development is similar. (Fullan, 1993). It is imperative, then, that superintendents understand that closeness does not mean control, and that autonomy does not mean neglect.

The third and fourth guidelines are closely related to each other and the third refers to the critical need to establish explicit selection criteria and procedures for promotion. This makes it crystal clear that only people who have already demonstrated initiative-taking, curriculum leadership, professional development (interactive forms) leadership, and the like need apply. Nothing conveys the message with greater force, as well as builds a critical mass of mutually-stimulating leaders, than decision after decision in which instructionally-oriented and skilled people are promoted.

Short-term and long-range leadership development programs make up the final essential component. School systems must invest in the mid- and long-range development of potential leaders, and in the continuing professional development of appointed leaders. Internships, short-term secondments and apprenticeships both within the system and external, such as to other boards, the faculties of education or the Ministry of Education and Training, are important. Mentoring and other structured peer-related approaches would be especially effective. For example, a newly-appointed vice-principal in one school can work with an experienced principal in another school, assisting the latter principal and teachers in assessing program implementation, or in designing and carrying out a professional growth program.

We see the powerful effects of this systemic approach over a period of years in the Durham Board of Education, which recently won the prestigious Bertelsmann Prize from Germany for being the most innovative school system in a world competition. In 1987, Durham was one of the least effective school systems as assessed in a government review. Less than ten years later, the Board was assessed as a model of effectiveness on the Bertelsmann criteria which included: innovation; innovative school leadership; participation of students, parents and other partners; evaluation and quality assurance. (Fullan et al, 1996). They accomplished this through the systematic, sustained use of the four guidelines just outlined.

Closeness does not mean control, and autonomy does not mean neglect.

The theme of this book, however, is not to wait for "system" solutions. To do so is to externalize the solution, risking further dependency. Principals, as moral change agents, cannot afford to wait for school systems to attain this level of involvement. Or perhaps more accurately, systems will only reach this level, through the day-to-day activities of individuals pushing in the other direction.

Perpetual Learning

Managing in a nonrational world means counting on our own selves.

The ultimate safeguard against empowered managers going too far off track is that they are perpetual learners. When it comes to learning, effective leaders are greedy.

Bennis and Nanus (1985) identified a number of common characteristics in their interviews with highly effective leaders. Those interviewed discussed a number of things they do, "but, above all, they talked about learning." (p. 188) Bennis and Nanus continue:

> Nearly all leaders are highly proficient in learning from experience. Most were able to identify a small number of mentors and key experiences that powerfully shaped their philosophies, personalities, and operating style ... Learning is the essential fuel for the leader, the source of high-octane energy that keeps up the momentum by continually sparking new understanding, new ideas, and new challenges. It is absolutely indispensable under today's conditions of rapid change and complexity. Very simply, those who do not learn do not long survive as leaders. (Bennis and Nanus, 1985:188)

Kelleher, Finestone, and Lowy (1986) provide further insights into "managerial learning." In a study of 43 managers, they were able to divide the group into high, medium, and low learners based on an index of seven factors. They found interesting patterns of situations related to high learning — in particular, a combination of freedom, stress, and support. To highlight a few of the factors found in the study, the extent to which the manager was in a situation of expected innovation and latitude, supervisory support and supervisory pressure was correlated with higher learning. Kelleher and his colleagues also found that high learners experienced more stress.

Block describes the relationship between learning and stress as "moving toward tension:"

> Almost every important learning experience we have ever had has been stressful. Those issues that create stress for us give us clues about the uncooked seeds within us that need our attention. Stress and anxiety are an indication that we are living our lives and making choices. The entrepreneurial approach is to view tension as a vehicle for discovery. Dissatisfied customers teach us how to do business. People who do not use our services teach us how to sell. (Block, 1987:191)

Too much stress is a bad thing, but so is too little. Joy and stress not only can go together, but always coexist in high performers. (Hanson, 1985)

The advice for principals, in a nutshell, is to get into the habit of and situations for constant learning. Skill and know-how are as important as attitude. This means access to new ideas and situations, active experimentation, examination of analogous and dissimilar organizations, reflective practice, collegial learning, coaching in relation to practice and more. (Schon, 1987) Principals, as perpetual learners, are constantly reaching out for new ideas, seeing what they can learn from others and testing themselves against external standards.

Principals can make even more long-lasting contributions, by broadening the base of leadership of those with whom they work — teachers, parents, students. The other two books in the trilogy provide a series of guidelines for principals and teachers to establish wide-ranging leadership capacity which will make the goal of continuous improvement more reachable.

Organizations do not get healthy by themselves, and we all would be extremely lucky if our organization got healthy through someone else's efforts other than our own. Managing in a nonrational world means counting on our own selves:

> This is the true joy in life, the being used for a purpose recognized by yourself as a mighty one; the being a force of nature instead of a feverish selfish little clod of ailments and grievances complaining that the world will not devote itself to making you happy; I want to be thoroughly used up when I die, for the harder I work the more I live. I

rejoice in life for its own sake. Life is no "brief candle" to me. It is a sort of splendid torch which I have got hold of for the moment, and I want to make it burn as brightly as possible before handing it on to future generations (from Shaw's *Man and Superman* quoted in Bennis and Nanus)

Paradoxically, counting on oneself for a good cause in a highly interactive organization is the key to fundamental organizational change. People change organizations. The starting point is not system change, or change in those around us, but taking action ourselves. The challenge is to improve education in the only way it can be — through the day-to-day actions of empowered individuals. This is what's worth fighting for in the school principalship.

The challenge is to improve education in the only way it can be — through the day-to-day actions of empowered individuals.

References

Bennis, W. and Nanus, B. (1985). *Leaders.* New York, NY: Harper & Row.

Block, P. (1987) *The empowered manager.* San Francisco, CA: Jossey-Bass.

Champy, J. (1995). *Reengineering management.* New York, NY: Harper Collins.

Christensen, G. (1994). *The role of the principal in transforming accelerated schools.* Unpublished doctoral dissertation, Stanford University.

Dolan, P. (1994). *Restructuring our schools.* Kansas City, MO: Systems & Organizations.

Drucker, P. (1985). *Innovation and entrepreneurship.* New York, NY: Harper & Row.

Edu-Con. (1984). *The role of the public school principal in the Toronto Board of Education.* Toronto, ON: Edu-Con of Canada.

Epstein, J. (1995). "School/family/community partnerships", *Phi Delta Kappan*, Vol.76, pp 701-712.

Evans, R. (1996). *The human side of school change.* San Francisco, CA: Jossey-Bass.

Farson, R. (1996). *Management of the absurd.* New York, NY: Simon & Schuster.

Fullan, M. (1993). *Change forces.* London, U.K: Falmer Press.

Fullan, M. (1994). "Coordinating top-down and bottom-up strategies for educational reform." In R. Elmore & S. Fuhrman (Eds.), *The governance of curriculum.* Alexandria, VA: Association for Supervision & Curriculum, pp. 186-202.

Fullan, M. (1993). Coordinating school and district development in restructuring. In J. Murphy & P. Hallinger (Eds.), *Restructuring schooling: Learning from ongoing efforts.* Newbury Park, CA: Sage, pp. 143-164.

Fullan, M., Alberts, B., Lieberman, A. & Zywine, J. (1996). *Report of the Country Expert Commission, Canada/United States of America.* Germany: C. Bertelsmann Foundation.

Fullan, M. & Hargreaves, A. (1991, 1996). *What's worth fighting for in your school?* Toronto, ON: Ontario Public School Teachers' Federation; New York, NY: Teachers College Press.

Gitlin, A. & Margonis, F. (1995). "The political aspect of reform: Teacher resistance as good sense." *American Journal of Education*, Vol. 103, pp 377-405.

Hanson, P. (1985) *The joy of stress.* Toronto, ON: Hanson Stress Management Organization.

Hargreaves, A. & Fullan, M. (*forthcoming*). *What's worth fighting for out there?* Toronto, ON: Ontario Public School Teachers' Federation; New York, NY: Teachers College Press.

Henry, M. (1996). *Parent-school collaboration: Feminist organizational structures and school leadership.* Albany, NY: State University of New York Press.

Kelleher, D., Finestone, P. & Lowy, A. (1986). "Managerial learning: first notes from an unstudied frontier," *Group & Organization Studies*, VII, pp. 169-202.

Lortie, D. (1987). *Built-in tendencies toward stabilizing the principal's role.* Paper presented at the annual meeting of the American Education Research Association.

Louis, K. (1989). "The role of school districts in school improvement." In M. Holmes, K. Leithwood & D. Musella (Eds.), *Educational policy for effective schools.* Toronto, ON: OISE Press, (pp. 145-167).

Maurer, R. (1996). *Beyond the wall of resistance.* Austin, TX: Bard Books

Miles, M. (1987). *Practical guidelines for school administrators: How to get there.* Paper presented at the annual meeting of the American Education Research Association.

Mintzberg, H. (1994) *The rise and fall of strategic planning* New York, NY: Free Press.

Newmann, F. & Wehlage, G. (1995) *Successful school restructuring.* Madison, WI: Center on Organization and Restructuring of Schools.

Ontario Royal Commission on Learning. (1994). *For the love of learning,* Vol. I — V. Toronto, ON: Queen's Printer.

Patterson, J., Purkey, S., and Parker, J. (1986). *Productive school systems for a nonrational world.* Alexandria, VA: Association for Supervision and Curriculum Development.

Prestine, N. (1994). *Ninety degrees from everywhere: New understandings of the principal's role in a restructuring essential school.* Paper presented at the annual meeting of the American Education Research Association.

Rothschild, J. (1990). *Feminist values and the democratic management of work organizations.* Paper presented at the 12th World Congress of Sociology, Madrid, Spain.

Sarason, S. (1982) *The culture of the school and the problem of change.* (2nd edition), Boston, MA: Allyn &: Bacon.

Sarason, S. (1995). *Parent involvement and the political principal.* San Francisco, CA: Jossey-Bass.

Schon, D. (1987). *Educating the reflective practitioner.* San Francisco, CA: Jossey-Bass.

Senge, P. (1990). *The fifth discipline.* New York, NY: Doubleday.

Stacey, R. (1996) *Complexity and creativity in organizations.* San Francisco, CA: Berrett-Koehler Publishers.

Sullivan, G. & Harper, M. (1996). *Hope is not a method: What business leaders can learn from the American Army.* New York, NY: Random House.

Wylie, C. (1995). *School-site management: Some lessons from New Zealand.* Paper presented at the annual meeting of the American Educational Research Association.

About the Author

Michael Fullan is the Dean of the newly formed Ontario Institute for Studies in Education of the University of Toronto. An innovator and leader in teacher education, he has developed a number of partnerships designed to bring about major school improvement and educational reform. He participated as researcher, consultant, trainer, and policy advisor on a wide range of educational change projects with school systems, teachers' federations, research development institutes, and government agencies in Canada and internationally. Michael Fullan has published widely on the topic of educational change. His most recent books are *Change Forces: Probing the Depths of Educational Reform* (Falmer Press), *The New Meaning of Educational Change* (Teachers College Press), and the two other books in the WHAT'S WORTH FIGHTING FOR? series, both written with Andy Hargreaves: *What's Worth Fighting For in Your School?* and *What's Worth Fighting For "Out There"?*